Divine Encounters with Sai

Orange Books Publication

1st Floor, Rajhans Arcade, Mall Road, Kohka, Bhilai, Chhattisgarh 490020
Website: www.orangebooks.in

© Copyright, 2025, Author

All rights reserved. No part of this book may be reproduced, stored in a retrieval system, or transmitted, in any form by any means, electronic, mechanical, magnetic, optical, chemical, manual, photocopying, recording or otherwise, without the prior written consent of its writer.

First Edition, 2025
ISBN: 978-93-6554-135-9

DIVINE ENCOUNTERS WITH
SAI

A MOTHER'S JOURNEY OF MIRACLES,
FAITH, AND BLESSINGS

VANDANA RAWAT

Orange Books Publication
www.orangebooks.in

Dedication

To my beloved daughters,

who mean the world to me.

You are my inspiration, my joy,

and my greatest blessing.

With all my love, always.

Preface

This book is a heartfelt journey of unwavering faith, challenges, and divine intervention. As a mother to a beautiful 19-year-old daughter with autism, life has been an extraordinary tapestry of struggles, love, and miracles. While navigating the complexities of raising a child with special needs, I often found myself overwhelmed, searching for answers, strength, and hope. It was during these moments that Sai Baba entered our lives, not as a distant deity but as a constant guide, companion, and source of solace.

This book is not merely about spirituality—it is about the transformative power of faith, patience (Saburi), and surrendering to the divine. It is about the small miracles that shaped my life and brought remarkable changes to my daughter. Despite her challenges, my daughter's profound and pure devotion to Sai Baba—offering prasad every Thursday without fail—taught me that faith knows no barriers, whether mental, emotional, or physical.

Through my story, I hope to share the light and grace we have received so that others who face their trials may find comfort and inspiration. This book is for parents, caregivers, and anyone who believes or wishes to believe in miracles. It is my humble attempt to show

that Sai Baba's presence is real, his love is boundless, and through him, even the most challenging journeys can lead to peace, progress, and divine blessings.

Interface (Introduction)

A Journey of Faith, Miracles, And Blessings

In the tapestry of life, we all encounter moments that test the very fabric of our being—challenges that leave us questioning our strength, our purpose, and at times, even our faith. My moment of reckoning came when I began to comprehend the unique path my daughter would tread as a child with autism.

As a mother, I longed for her to laugh freely, to grow confidently, and to soar beyond the barriers life had placed before her. But life, in its unpredictable way, had other plans. There were days when despair wrapped around me like an unforgiving storm. I felt powerless and adrift—until Sai Baba entered our lives.

It wasn't a thunderous awakening or a blinding epiphany. Sai Baba came gently, like a soft whisper that settled into my heart. Every Thursday, I began visiting His temple. I started small—offering food, clothes, or anything that could ease the lives of those in need. With each humble act of devotion, something began to shift.

Miracles began to weave themselves into our story. Small progress in my daughter's development that once seemed impossible now started becoming reality. I discovered reservoirs of strength within me that I had never known. And amidst the chaos, a profound sense of peace found its way into my heart, with the arrival of my second daughter.

My daughter, despite her condition, embraced Sai Baba in a way that left me speechless. With the innocence of a child, she began offering prasad every Thursday—a ritual that became her sacred connection to the divine. Watching her find joy, purpose, and faith became my miracle.

"Divine Encounters with Sai" is a testament to these moments of grace and surrender. It is a chronicle of the divine interventions, the healing power of faith, and the profound lessons I learned as a mother, a seeker, and a believer.

Through these pages, I invite you into our journey—a journey where faith turned tears into hope, where surrender birthed miracles, and where love revealed its limitless power.

This book is my heartfelt offering to every parent, caregiver, or soul who has ever felt overwhelmed by life's trials. May it remind you to hold on, to believe in the whispers of the divine, and to trust in the timing of the universe.

Sai Baba's presence is real—if you open your heart and listen, you too will hear, His gentle whispers of love and faith.

Contents

Chapter 1
    The Call Of Sai 1

Chapter 2
    Signs Of His Presence 6

Chapter 3
    Hope Amidst Despair 11

Chapter 4
    A Test Of Faith 17

Chapter 5
    From Guilt to Grace 23

Chapter 6
    Miracle Of Faith 30

Chapter 7
    The Day We Waited For 37

Chapter 8
    Whispers Of Faith And Connections 42

Chapter 9
A Guiding Light In The Storm 48

Chapter 10
The Second Chance At Parenthood 54

Chapter 11
Battling The Odds with Silent Courage 60

Chapter 12
A Divine Encounter 66

Chapter 13
The Mystical Prasad Connection 72

Chapter 14
The Awaited Blessings 78

Chapter 1
The Call Of Sai

It was a cold, bleak December day in Delhi, and darkness seemed to hang heavy over my life. That day, my daughter was diagnosed with Autism. I was devastated. She wasn't social, she recoiled from textures, she couldn't walk, and worst of all, she couldn't communicate. As her mother, I felt utterly drained—broken, lost, and with no idea of what to do next. Sitting at her therapy center, my heart ached, the weight of helplessness suffocating me. That was when I met another mother, her child too was having mild learning difficulties.

We began talking, two strangers bound by similar pain. As we shared our challenges, she spoke of an extraordinary encounter that changed her life—a story filled with the grace of Sai Baba. She told me about a revered Sai temple in Delhi, where she experienced a miracle that defied logic.

Her story began with her struggle to conceive. Years of endless medical treatments and dashed hopes had left her in despair. She had all but given up. Then, someone suggested she visit the Sai temple and pray. Clinging to a fragile thread of hope, she began visiting the temple regularly. Six months later, the impossible happened—she conceived. However, her pregnancy was high-risk, and her doctor advised complete bed rest.

One night, during those fraught months, she dreamt of Sai Baba calling her to the temple. The dream was so vivid, so intense, that she could not ignore it. Despite her condition, she went to the temple the next morning. As she climbed the stairs, fear gripped her heart. It felt as if something was slipping away from her, like her baby was in peril. Terrified, she closed her eyes and whispered a desperate prayer: "Baba, please help me. Don't let me lose this child. This might be my only chance at becoming a mother. Please, Baba, save my baby."

In that moment of despair, she felt a warm, gentle hand holding hers. Startled, she opened her eyes to see an elderly man standing beside her. His voice was calm, and soothing as he said, "Utho beta, chalo mere saath mandir chalo (Rise, my child. Come with me to the temple)." Without hesitation, she let him guide her up the stairs, her fear melting away with every step. But when they reached the temple hall, she realized the old man was no longer with her. Confused, she searched for him everywhere, but he was gone. It was then she understood—he was none other than Sai Baba himself. Overcome with emotion, she wept, her tears a mixture of awe and gratitude.

Meanwhile, her mother-in-law, who had been waiting below with the prasad, rushed to her side, alarmed at her tears. Together, they hurried to her gynaecologist. What happened next was nothing short of miraculous. The doctor, who had earlier warned of complications, now found everything perfectly normal. The baby was safe and thriving. In fact, the doctor was so astonished by the sudden improvement that she allowed the mother to resume her daily activities. The rest of her pregnancy progressed smoothly, and in time, she gave birth to a healthy baby. Later, she even went on to have a second child.

As she narrated her story, I found myself overwhelmed with emotion. Tears streamed down my face as I listened, her words igniting a spark of hope in my heart. We embraced, two mothers united in a moment of shared humanity, and we cried together—tears of pain, faith, and perhaps, of a future yet unseen.

That night, as I lay in bed, her story replayed in my mind. I couldn't shake the feeling that Sai Baba was calling me too. It felt as though her story was a message meant for me, a gentle nudge toward his boundless ocean of grace. There was a magnetism in my heart, a pull I could not resist.

That was the moment my journey toward Sai Baba began, a journey that would lead me to solace, strength, and the embrace of his divine love.

Chapter 2
Signs Of His Presence

The week that followed was chaotic, consumed by the endless race to get my daughter's assessments done, from speech therapy sessions to occupational therapy appointments. The emotional turmoil I had been experiencing seemed to linger, and amidst the hustle, one thought was persistent—Baba. That night the lady's story kept replaying in my mind like a song stuck getting repeated.

Two weeks passed by, and it was the Thursday of the third week. I was on my way to Connaught Place in New Delhi, weaving through the bustling streets when my car passed the famous Sai Baba temple on that road. My heart suddenly felt heavy, as if the air had thickened around me. Flashes of that story, the emotions, and the uneasiness from the night at the therapy centre came rushing back. A strange voice within me whispered, almost pleading, "Go to Baba's shelter." But I ignored it—again.

Days went by, and this unexplainable connection with Baba began unfolding more vividly. His presence seemed to follow me everywhere. I started noticing Baba's photo in places I never expected—on walls, shop signs, vehicles, and even in random advertisements. It was as if the universe was conspiring to remind me of Him, as though He was reaching out, trying to grab my attention.

There was a constant tug at my subconscious mind, urging me to acknowledge His presence. It wasn't loud or intrusive—it was gentle, like a soft whisper. But my conscious mind wasn't ready to listen. I kept brushing off the signs, convincing myself that it was just my imagination. Yet, deep within, I knew it wasn't. I could feel Him, almost as if He were beside me, silently watching over me and my daughter.

One evening, I was sitting with my father-in-law. He was a quiet, wise man with a calm aura that always brought comfort to our home. Though I had noticed a large photo of Sai Baba in his room before, we had never spoken about it. That evening, he must have sensed my distress. With a gentle smile, he walked towards me, holding a small bottle with a blue cap.

"Beta(child)" he said softly, his voice filled with warmth, "I can see that you are troubled. Take this Vibhuti and apply it to your eyes and tongue. It will help."

I hesitated, unsure of what he was offering me. The bottle contained ashes—ordinary-looking, yet they felt extraordinary at that moment. Despite my doubts, something in his tone gave me the faith to trust him. I did as he said. As I applied the Vibhuti, I felt an inexplicable calmness wash over me.

Curiosity got the better of me, and I asked, "Papaji, what is this?"

His answer made my heart skip a beat. "Beta, this is Sai Baba's Vibhuti."

Sai Baba again. The words echoed in my mind, and a sense of wonder gripped me. Was this yet another sign? My thoughts were interrupted as he began to share a story—a story that changed my perspective forever.

He told me about his maternal uncle, who had once experienced a miraculous intervention by Sai Baba. Papaji explained that his uncle and some relatives were traveling to Shirdi when their minibus's brakes failed on a dangerous, winding road. As the bus started rolling backward toward a deep pit, panic ensued. Everyone screamed in terror, convinced their end was near. In a moment of desperation, his uncle cried out, "Baba, please save us! We are coming to see You!"

Just as the bus was about to plunge into the pit, it stopped abruptly. A large boulder had lodged itself under the back tire, halting the vehicle and saving everyone. Papaji's voice trembled slightly as he spoke, his faith evident in every word. "Since that day, I have believed in Baba. This vibhuti was given to me by my uncle. Whenever I feel low, I apply it, and it brings me peace."

As he finished his story, I sat there in silence, overwhelmed by a mix of emotions—gratitude, awe, and a growing sense of belief. It was then I realized that all these signs weren't coincidences. Baba was reaching out to me, calling me to His shelter.

The following Thursday, I couldn't resist anymore. I visited the humble Sai temple in my locality. The moment I stepped inside, a wave of calm engulfed me. The energy was magnetic, almost divine. When I stood before Baba's statue, tears welled up in my eyes. It was a feeling I couldn't put into words—peace, comfort, and a deep connection that I had been yearning for without even knowing it.

At that moment, I knew. Baba had been with me all along, guiding me through my struggles, waiting for me to turn to Him. And now, I was ready to embrace Him completely.

Chapter 3
Hope Amidst Despair

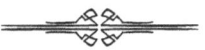

Days turned into weeks, and visiting Baba's temple every Thursday became a part of my life. It wasn't a planned ritual; it just happened, as though my soul craved that peace, that connection. Life was moving at an unrelenting pace. My days and nights blurred together as I tirelessly worked toward helping my daughter—hoping, praying, fighting to get her to walk, to speak, and to simply move past her challenges.

Her fear of textures was a constant barrier. The thought of taking steps terrified her, and each attempt seemed to make things worse. It felt as though the world had paused, with every moment filled with her struggles and my helplessness.

Around that time, my younger sister, who happens to be a physiotherapist, came to stay with us. She was interning at a renowned hospital in Delhi, and her presence felt like a much-needed anchor in my stormy sea. I confided in her, pouring out all my fears and anxieties, hoping she might have a solution. She suggested visiting one of the most reputed hospitals in Delhi—a place which is known for its exceptional care and expertise.

The following week, we managed to get an appointment. The day finally arrived, and as fate would have it, it was a Thursday. With equal parts of hope and dread, I took my daughter to the hospital.

The scene there was overwhelming. It wasn't just a hospital; it felt like an ocean of human pain and resilience. The outpatient department was teeming with parents and children, some who had come from faraway villages, others visibly poor but holding onto the hope of giving their child a better chance at life.

The weight of the atmosphere crushed me. My heart thudded painfully in my chest, and I could feel my nerves unraveling. My sister went off to complete the formalities, asking me to wait. But sitting there, amidst the silent cries and anxious faces, was unbearable. Every ticking second stretched into eternity. I looked around at the exhausted faces, at the helplessness in their eyes, and it mirrored my own.

Half an hour passed, but it felt like a lifetime. When my sister finally returned, she informed me that we would have to wait another hour to meet the doctor. I couldn't bear it anymore. Tears welled up, and I broke down. "I can't do this," I sobbed. "I just want to leave. I can't take it anymore."

My sister held my hand firmly, her voice calm but insistent. "We've come this far. Let's wait, let's get her checked. It's important."

Her words, her presence, somehow kept me going. I paced the hallway, unable to sit, my heart pounding with an intensity that almost scared me. I whispered silent prayers, pleading for strength, for hope, for a miracle.

Finally, our turn came. As we entered the consultation room, I felt a strange heaviness, like the weight of all my fears pressing down on me. The doctor greeted us with a warm smile. She looked to be in her early thirties, her voice gentle and reassuring.

I sat there in silence, unable to speak, afraid that if I opened my mouth, the storm within me would pour out uncontrollably. My sister, my rock, came to my rescue once again. She explained everything to the doctor—my daughter's fear of textures, her inability to walk, and all the therapies we had tried.

The doctor listened patiently, nodding as she examined my daughter. She performed a series of physical tests and then turned to us with a calm, comforting expression. "There's no issue with her legs," she said softly. "She just needs time and a little encouragement. She will walk soon. Don't worry."

Her words were like a breath of fresh air. A wave of relief swept over me, washing away the suffocating fear that had gripped me for so long. My heart, which had been pounding incessantly, began to calm. My mind, which had been clouded with anxiety, started to clear.

I felt an overwhelming urge to thank her. I bent forward, gratitude filling every fibre of my being. And then, as my eyes fell on her, I noticed something that left me utterly astonished—she was wearing a Sai Baba locket.

Time seemed to stand still. A wave of emotion surged through me, a mix of amazement, gratitude, and an inexplicable sense of connection. I couldn't speak, but my heart felt as if it was shouting, "Baba, you're here! You've always been here!"

It wasn't just a locket. It was a sign, a reminder, a miracle of faith. Baba had been guiding me all along, reassuring me in ways I couldn't comprehend, showing me that he was beside me and my daughter, every step of the way.

That day, I walked out of the hospital with more than just a sense of relief. I walked out with faith—a deep, unshakable faith that no matter how difficult the journey might be, Baba was watching over us. Always.

Chapter 4
A Test of Faith

After returning from the hospital, I was filled with a sense of relief and hope. It felt as though a heavy burden had been lifted from my shoulders, and my heart was lighter than it had been in weeks. The first thought that came to my mind was to visit Sai Baba's temple to thank Him for this glimmer of hope. That day, everything felt different. I gave my daughter a bath, prepared food, and made 'Sooji ka Halwa'(a sweet) as an offering. It felt as though positivity was raining all around me, and my heart was brimming with gratitude.

The evening sun was beginning to set as I stepped into the temple. The moment I entered the hall, I was overwhelmed by the divine aura of Baba's idol. Dressed in yellow gota-patti robes with a shining mukut (crown) and a garland of roses, the idol exuded serenity and power. I couldn't help but sit down on the carpet spread across the temple floor, gazing at Baba's idol in awe. It was as though His eyes were looking directly into mine, offering solace that words could never express.

As I waited for the priest to come and accept the offerings, I opened my Sai Chalisa and began reading. The words, though familiar, felt more meaningful that day, as if they were wrapping me in comfort. When I finished the last line, I closed my eyes and spoke to Baba from the depths of my heart:

"Baba, thank you for the hope You've given me today. I don't have enough words to express my gratitude, but I must ask—why me? Why this test, Baba? I am Your child, and I have complete faith in You. I need Your love, Your guidance. My daughter needs You. These challenges are breaking her and our family. Please come to us, Baba. Please help us."

As I poured my heart out, the priest arrived, and the devotees began forming a line to offer their prasad. I stood in the queue, clutching my offering tightly, still feeling the weight of my prayers.

Days passed, and life settled back into its rhythm. My younger sister, who is a physiotherapist, continued working tirelessly with my daughter. She created textured surfaces around the house to help my daughter overcome her fear of walking, but something still wasn't working. Progress felt slow, and I could feel my hope starting to waver.

One Thursday evening, I went to the market to buy sesame seeds and jaggery for Baba, as I wanted to offer Him til gur. The weather was unusual—dark clouds loomed overhead, and a few drops of rain began to fall, even though it was October. Lost in my thoughts, I wandered through the small shops, trying to gather everything I needed.

At one shop, I noticed an old man standing beside me. He wore simple white clothes and had a white cloth draped over his head. In a soft voice, he said,

"Child, give me something. At least a ten-rupee note."

I didn't even turn to look at him. Like so many others begging on the streets, I assumed he was just another needy person. Annoyed, I waved him away and moved to another shop. But he followed me. At the next shop, he again asked, "Child, give me something. At least a ten-rupee note."

Distracted by my own worries, I ignored him once more and walked away. I don't even remember looking at his face. I completed my shopping, visited the temple to offer my prasad, and went home, not giving the incident another thought.

Weeks went by, and I fell back into my routine. My daughter's progress was slow, and with each passing day, my hope began to fade. One Thursday morning, five weeks after my visit to the hospital, I stood in front of the small temple in my home, offering prayers to Sai Baba. I had cooked a meal, as I usually did, to donate to someone in need.

That day, my heart was heavy with sadness. It had been weeks, and my daughter still wasn't walking. The hope I had felt at the hospital seemed like a distant memory. With tears streaming down my face, I closed my eyes and spoke to Baba again:

"Baba, where did I go wrong? Why are You not helping me? Why are You not coming to me when I need You the most?"

As I stood there in despair, a voice echoed in my mind, soft but clear:

"I came, my child. I came to help you, but you did not recognize me."

I opened my eyes, startled. My mind raced as I tried to understand the meaning of those words. And then, like a flash of lightning, it hit me—the old man in the market! The man who had asked for just ten rupees.

My heart sank as the realization dawned on me. That wasn't just any man. That was Baba Himself. Baba had come to me, and I had failed to recognize Him. The weight of my mistake crushed me. My knees felt weak, and my mind was consumed by guilt.

"I ignored Baba," I whispered to myself, over and over. "I ignored Baba."

It was as if I had failed the ultimate test of faith. Baba had come to me, and I had turned Him away. The thought hammered at my heart, leaving me drowning in sorrow and regret.

That day, I learned a lesson that will stay with me forever: Faith is not just about prayers and rituals—it's about recognizing the divine in unexpected moments and places. And in that moment of realization, I promised Baba that I would never let doubt cloud my faith again.

Chapter 5
From Guilt to Grace

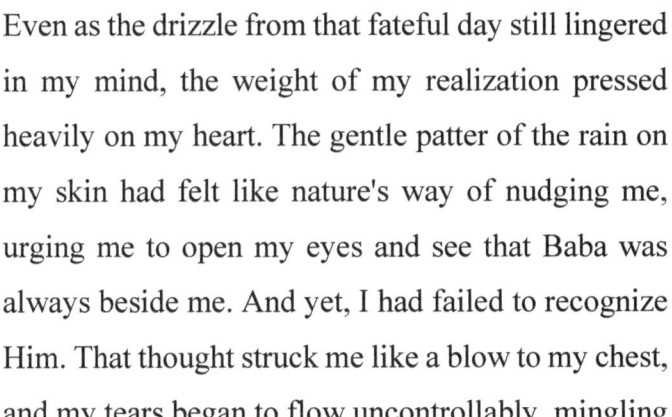

Even as the drizzle from that fateful day still lingered in my mind, the weight of my realization pressed heavily on my heart. The gentle patter of the rain on my skin had felt like nature's way of nudging me, urging me to open my eyes and see that Baba was always beside me. And yet, I had failed to recognize Him. That thought struck me like a blow to my chest, and my tears began to flow uncontrollably, mingling with the memory of that rain.

I felt hollow, consumed by regret and sorrow. A deep stillness settled over the day as if the world had turned gray, mirroring the despair that had enveloped me. I couldn't shake the image of that beggar's eyes—the kindness, the quiet plea, the divine presence I had ignored. My chest ached with guilt, and the heaviness in my soul made it difficult to even breathe.

Unable to bear the pain, I collapsed onto my bed, clutching my pillow as if it could absorb the storm inside me. My sobs were unrelenting, each one a plea for forgiveness—for a chance to undo my mistake. The hours slipped by unnoticed as I lay there, drowning in my remorse. The light of the afternoon dimmed into the shadows of evening, but the darkness in my heart remained unchanged.

As night approached, I forced myself to get up and go about my chores, though my movements were mechanical, my mind elsewhere. It was Thursday, a day I had always dedicated to visiting the Sai temple. Despite my broken spirit, I decided to stick to the routine, as if the familiar act of devotion might bring some solace.

With trembling hands and a heavy heart, I stepped into the temple. The familiar sight of Baba's idol greeted me, His serene expression unchanged, as though He had been patiently waiting for me to return. The sight broke something deep within me, and I sank to the carpeted floor in front of Him, unable to contain the storm of emotions any longer.

"Baba," I whispered through my tears, "I failed You. You came to me, and I didn't see You. How could I not recognize You, Baba? How could I let You down like this?" My voice cracked as the words spilled out, unfiltered and raw. "I don't deserve Your compassion, but I beg You—please don't turn away from me. Please come back to me. I need You now more than ever."

The temple was filled with the soft hum of devotees chanting *"Om Sai Ram,"* but to me, the world seemed silent, save for the sound of my own heart breaking. My tears blurred my vision as I gazed at Baba's idol, silently pleading for a sign, for some reassurance that I hadn't lost Him forever.

It was then that the temple priest, Panditji, approached me. He had seen me many times before during my visits, but today, he must have noticed the despair written all over my face. His voice was gentle, almost fatherly, as he asked, "Child, what troubles you so deeply today? Tell me, what has happened?"

Through my tears, I told him everything—the beggar, the realization, the unbearable guilt. As I spoke, the weight of my emotions spilled out, leaving me trembling and vulnerable. Panditji listened quietly, his expression calm and understanding. When I finished, he gave me a kind smile and said something that struck a chord deep within me.

"Baba chooses whom He wants to visit," he began, his voice steady and soothing. "When He comes to you, it is not because you have done something wrong or right. It is because He sees your heart and knows your pain. Do not feel guilty, child. Instead, feel blessed that Baba chose you. His ways are mysterious, but His love is boundless."

His words, though comforting, did little to ease my torment. "But Panditji," I whispered, "I let Him down. I didn't recognize Him. What if He doesn't come back? What if I've lost my chance forever?"

Panditji placed a reassuring hand on my shoulder. "Baba never abandons those who seek Him with faith," he said. Then, reaching for a nearby shelf, he pulled out a small red book with silver lettering: the *Sai Satcharitra*.

"Take this," he said, handing me the book. "This is Baba's life and teachings. Read it with devotion, and you will find the answers you seek. Baba always said two things: *Shraddha* (faith) and *Saboori* (patience). Hold on to these, and you will see His presence in every corner of your life."

I clutched the book tightly, as though it were a lifeline. "Will reading this bring Baba back to me?" I asked, my voice trembling with both hope and fear.

Panditji smiled. "Baba is already with you," he said. "Reading this book will not bring Him to you—it will help you see that He has been with you all along. Trust in His timing, child. Everything happens as per His divine will."

As I prepared to leave, Panditji placed a hand on my head and recited words that would stay with me forever: "Man ka ho toh accha, aur man ka na ho toh aur bhi accha, kyunki jo hota hai woh prabhu ichha anusar hota hai. Aur koi pita apne bachche ke saath kabhi galat nahi hone deta."

If things happen as you wish, it's good. But if they don't, it's even better, because it happens as per God's will. And no father ever lets harm come to His child.

Those words echoed in my mind as I walked home, clutching the *Sai Satcharitra* and prasad in my hands. The weight of guilt in my heart began to lift, replaced by a flicker of hope. That evening, as I opened the book and began to read, I felt a strange sense of peace wash over me. It was as though Baba was sitting beside me, guiding me with every word.

At that moment, I realized that my journey with Baba was only beginning. My tears of despair had turned into tears of faith, and for the first time in days,

I felt a glimmer of light in the darkness. I vowed to rebuild my connection with Baba, one prayer, one act of devotion, one step at a time.

Chapter 6
Miracle Of Faith

Days turned into weeks, and I started reading the *Saicharitra* whenever I could steal a moment from my daily routine. With every page I read, I found myself sinking deeper into faith and patience in Baba—*Shraddha* and *Saboori*. Each reading was like peeling back a new layer of understanding. Spiritual insights that I had never imagined began to reveal themselves to me, filling my heart with peace and clarity.

The *Saicharitra* became more than just a book—it became a guide to my soul. I slowly realized that life doesn't unfold randomly; every moment, every joy, and every sorrow is written by God with a purpose.

And the more I thought about it, the more I began to understand: that we are chosen for certain journeys because God sees something special in us—strength, courage, resilience.

One day, as I sat in reflection, a thought came to me like a gentle whisper: my daughter wasn't just a challenge to bear or a responsibility to shoulder. She was a divine blessing, a pure angel sent by God Himself. And if God entrusts His angels only to the strongest, then He must have chosen me for her because He believed I was capable of giving her the love and care she deserved. This realization filled me with an unshakable sense of purpose, and I held her even closer to my heart.

Amid the whirlwind of therapy sessions for my daughter, daily chores, and reading *Saicharitra*, time flew by, and soon it was Makar Sankranti. This festival, in our tradition, is a time to donate to the less fortunate and begin anew with hope and kindness. I busied myself with preparations—planning what we would donate and gathering the items.

The day before the festival, I decided to buy blankets for donation. January in Delhi is bone-chillingly cold, and I thought blankets would provide warmth and comfort to those in need. After running errands all day, I returned home exhausted but content. After serving dinner and tidying up the house, I fell into bed, utterly drained.

That night, something incredible happened. In my dream, I felt a soft, warm light on my face. I heard a voice, gentle and reassuring, that said, "I will come to meet you soon." It was Baba's voice.

I woke up suddenly, startled and confused. Was it a dream? Or had I truly felt His presence? For a few moments, I sat there, frozen, unable to make sense of what had just happened. The clock read 6 a.m., and I decided to shake off my confusion and start the day.

The morning passed in a blur of rituals and preparations. My husband was leaving for work, and I had to take my daughter to her therapy session. We completed the pooja hurriedly, but before he left, I reminded him that we would go to the temple in the evening to donate the blankets. He nodded and promised to come home early.

That evening, as promised, my husband, daughter, and I went to the Sai temple. Although it wasn't a Thursday, the temple was teeming with people. Perhaps the festival had drawn the crowd. I carried the bag of blankets, but as I looked at the sea of faces, a pang of worry crept into my heart. I only had 11 blankets, and there were far more people waiting for donations.

I approached the *panditji* and shared my concern. He listened patiently and reassured me, saying, "Don't worry. I will send *sevaks* to help you distribute the blankets. It will be easier for you to manage, especially with your little one." Grateful for his kindness, I nodded, and the *sevaks* led us to the temple entrance, where the donations were being distributed to avoid overcrowding inside.

The distribution began, and in mere seconds, ten blankets were gone. Only one remained in my hands. A crowd of children surrounded me, each pleading for the last blanket. My heart ached as I tried to decide who needed it the most.

Suddenly, an old woman emerged from the crowd. Her face was weathered, yet there was a serenity about her that caught my attention. She looked at me with kind, knowing eyes and said, "This blanket is for me. You told me you would give it to me, remember?"

Her words left me stunned. I didn't recall speaking to her before, yet her voice carried a certainty that silenced my doubts. Without hesitation, she gently took the blanket from my hands. Placing her hand on my head, she whispered a blessing. Then, with both hands raised, she blessed my daughter, who was cradled in my husband's arms.

Her touch was unlike anything I had ever felt before—soothing, divine, and filled with an unexplainable warmth. It was as though all the burdens I had been carrying silently in my heart were lifted in that single moment. I stood there, motionless, as she turned and walked into the temple.

Something compelled me to follow her. I told my husband to take our daughter to the car, assuring him I wouldn't take long. I stepped into the temple, searching for the old woman, but to my shock, she was nowhere to be found. I had seen her enter the temple hall, yet it was as though she had vanished into thin air.

Panicked, I approached *panditji*. "Did you see an old woman with a red blanket enter the temple just now?" I asked breathlessly. He looked at me, puzzled, and said, "No, I didn't see anyone like that. It's not possible for someone to come and go so quickly. There's only one entrance."

I felt a chill run down my spine. I searched every corner of the temple, but she was gone. Finally, the truth dawned on me—it wasn't an ordinary encounter. This was a *Sai Leela*. Baba Himself had come to accept my offering. The realization brought tears to my eyes and left me trembling with emotion.

I returned to *panditji* and recounted the entire incident. He listened intently, his face reflecting the awe I felt in my heart. Smiling, he handed me *prasad—chana* and *gur*—and said, "Baba has blessed you. He always answers those who call Him with unwavering faith. You are truly fortunate."

As I left the temple that evening, tears streamed down my face. My heart was full, my soul light. I knew, without a shadow of a doubt, that Baba had come to heal me, to bless my daughter, and to remind me that faith, when true and unshaken, always brings miracles.

Chapter 7
The Day We Waited For

After that night, life went on as usual. Our days were filled with therapies and endless routines. My sister diligently worked on my daughter's physiotherapy, helping her with walking exercises. Slowly but surely, my daughter began showing small signs of improvement. These tiny milestones meant the world to me, each one bringing hope and joy amidst the challenges.

Yet, amidst all this, there was a part of me that was engulfed in an indescribable state. It was as if my heart carried a weight I couldn't put into words. The face of the woman who vanished in the temple haunted me. Every time I closed my eyes to pray to

Sai Baba, her face would appear alongside his divine image. There was something extraordinary about her face—an unexplainable power, a divine presence that I could still feel. Even today, that face is etched in my memory, radiating a sense of peace and strength.

It was an ordinary Thursday evening when I returned from the Sai temple with prasad. As per our family ritual, I placed the prasad on the centre table in the drawing room. Our tradition was simple yet heartfelt—after offering prasad at the temple, we would prepare food for Sai Baba and then share it with someone in need. After the evening pooja, my father-in-law would apply vibhuti to all of us, a gesture that always filled the house with a sense of calm and devotion.

That day, after completing the pooja, my father-in-law applied vibhuti to each of us and then placed the blue-capped bottle of vibhuti on the centre table. I was in my room when I realized that I hadn't distributed the prasad to everyone. Feeling a pang of guilt, I went to the drawing room to fetch it.

What I saw there stopped me in my tracks. My daughter was standing near the table, holding the bottle of vibhuti in her tiny hands. To my shock, she had emptied the bottle into her hands and was rubbing the vibhuti all over herself—her face, her head, her arms. The sight was chaotic, and without thinking, I screamed, "Oh God, what are you doing?"

Hearing my voice, my father-in-law, mother-in-law, and others came rushing into the room. My father-in-law gestured for me to remain silent and said, "Let her be. Just watch."

What happened next was nothing short of a miracle.

With the bottle still clutched in one hand, my daughter steadied herself by holding the center table with her other hand. Slowly, with wobbly steps, she began to walk. I could barely breathe as I watched her cover the length of the corridor, her unsteady feet finding their way with each step. She made her way toward the small temple in the corner of our house. We followed her in silence, too overwhelmed to speak.

Reaching the temple, she placed the bottle of vibhuti gently on the floor in front of the idols. Then, turning around, she began to walk back, her little feet still shaky but determined. Her eyes found mine, and suddenly, she burst into giggles—a sound so pure and joyful that it filled the entire room.

She made her way to me, her laughter echoing as she reached my arms. I scooped her up and held her close, tears streaming down my face. Around me, I could see everyone crying—their faces were a mix of disbelief, gratitude, and overwhelming happiness. My daughter's giggles were like a symphony, drowning out all the struggles we had faced so far.

Words cannot describe what I felt at that moment. It was as if time stood still, and in that stillness, the universe gave us the miracle we had been praying for.

That day, we experienced a divine blessing, one that reaffirmed our faith and gave us renewed strength.

It was a day we had been waiting for—a day that reminded us that hope and love could create miracles.

Chapter 8
Whispers Of Faith And Connections

The joyous days had finally knocked on our hearts. My daughter was making progress—not just in her ability to walk, but in so many other areas of her life. Each small achievement she made felt like a celebration of hope. The positivity and motivation in our home were at an all-time high, and I could feel the negative thoughts about her future slowly dissolving into the background. My husband and I began to notice the changes in her, and those moments filled our hearts with a renewed sense of purpose and joy.

We took a big step and enrolled her in a nearby preschool. At first, she was heavily dependent on me for everything. But slowly, almost miraculously, she started doing small things on her own. These tiny victories, though they may seem ordinary to others, felt extraordinary to us. She was blossoming in ways we had never imagined, though we knew there was still a long road ahead. The speech therapist recommended that we work on her social skills and encouraged us to explore special education centres where she could better learn to connect with others.

This was a time in India when the understanding of autism was scarce. People often confused it with mental retardation, and the stigma was overwhelming. The lack of awareness created endless hurdles. I remember vividly how parents of other children would pull their kids away from playing with my daughter, whispering among themselves, as if she carried some invisible affliction. Their judgment stung deeply. My daughter wasn't what they thought—she had an above-average IQ, but no matter how much I wanted to explain, their closed minds wouldn't hear me. Frustration and depression began creeping back into my life, threatening to consume the fragile hope we had built.

As if this wasn't enough, life threw another challenge our way. My mother-in-law's health took a serious turn, and we had to admit her to the hospital. My days became a blur—rushing to my daughter's therapies, juggling household responsibilities, and spending nights at the hospital caring for my mother-in-law. Every moment felt like an uphill battle, yet somehow, I managed to hold everything together. But the struggle was real, and there were moments when I questioned how long I could keep going.

One Thursday, amidst this whirlwind of responsibilities, I visited the Sai Baba temple. I took prasad and packed some food for my mother-in-law before heading to the hospital. That night, after she had eaten and fallen asleep, I finally found a moment of quiet. I pulled out my Sai Satcharitra to read—a ritual that brought me solace no matter how chaotic life became.

As I read, the nurse entered the room to check my mother-in-law's vitals. She was a kind, soft-spoken Malayali woman in her early 40s. She noticed the book in my hand and smiled warmly. After finishing her work, I offered her some prasad, which she accepted graciously. Somehow, we always felt an unspoken connection, though I couldn't pinpoint why.

Later that night, around 11:30 PM, she returned to my room. It was a quiet night in the hospital, and she sat down beside me, curious about the book I was reading. We began to talk about Sai Baba, faith, and the miracles that come from trusting in the divine. Her words felt comforting, like an old friend's embrace. Yet, I hesitated to share anything about my daughter, fearing judgment.

But then, she shared a story of her own. She told me about her 12-year-old daughter and how, when her child was very young, she had visited the Sabarimala Ayyappa Temple with her father. This temple, nestled in the serene Periyar Tiger Reserve in Kerala, is one of India's most sacred pilgrimage sites, dedicated to Lord Ayyappa. She explained the unique tradition of the temple, where women of menstruating age (10-50 years) are not allowed entry due to the deity's celibacy.

She recalled how her daughter, during their visit, had suddenly bathed herself in the temple's sacred ash, the vibhuti. As her husband moved to stop her, the temple priest intervened and said, "Let her be. Let her do what she wants." Her story left me speechless.

For a moment, I couldn't think clearly. My mind raced back to the day my daughter had covered herself in vibhuti at home. Was this a coincidence, or was it something more? Was Sai Baba trying to tell me something through this conversation?

Before I could gather my thoughts or ask her anything further, the nurse was called away for duty on another floor. I sat there in the dimly lit hospital room, holding the Sai Satcharitra close to my heart, overwhelmed by what I had just heard.

It felt as though the universe was whispering to me, weaving together threads of hope, faith, and divine connection. That night, as I looked at my sleeping mother-in-law and thought about my daughter's journey, I couldn't help but wonder—was this Sai Baba's way of telling me to hold on, to believe, and to trust in his plan?

Chapter 9
A Guiding Light In The Storm

I couldn't sleep well that night. My mind was a whirlwind of emotions and thoughts, each more overpowering than the last. When I finally drifted off, it was already late, and by the time I woke up the next day, the clock showed 7:00 AM. This was unusual for me as I always woke up by 6:00 AM, and guilt gnawed at me for oversleeping.

I later found out that my mother-in-law, ever so thoughtful, had noticed my struggles to manage everything on my own. She had called the nurse early in the morning to help her, ensuring I could rest a bit longer. When I apologized for not being there, she simply smiled and reassured me, "It's okay, beta. You need rest too." Her kindness and understanding warmed my heart, though it didn't completely erase my guilt.

It was around that time that Papaji arrived at the hospital. He insisted that I leave and get some rest at home. Reluctantly, I took their leave, but my heart wasn't at peace. The conversation I'd had with the nurse the previous day kept replaying in my mind. As I stepped out of the room, I felt an inexplicable urgency to find her. I headed straight to the nursing station, but she wasn't there. I searched the entire hospital, my desperation growing with every step. Finally, someone told me her duty had ended, and she had left for the day.

Hearing this, a wave of disappointment washed over me. My mind wasn't ready to wait another day for the answers to the questions swirling inside me. Heavy-hearted and filled with curiosity, I returned home, my thoughts racing as I tried to make sense of it all.

Later that evening, after finishing my household chores, I packed dinner for Maaji with a renewed determination to meet the nurse. My excitement was palpable, and I almost ran toward the hospital, my steps fuelled by a mix of hope and anxiety. A strange thought kept haunting me—what if she disappeared just like the old lady at the temple had?

When I reached the hospital, I rushed to Maaji's room, set down the food, and asked Papaji to stay with her for a while. I then resumed my search for the nurse. This time, I caught a glimpse of her. She was busy attending to a patient, but just seeing her calmed the storm inside me. My heart, which had been racing as if it would leap out of my chest, finally slowed.

The nurse noticed me, and her warm, reassuring smile worked like a balm to my restless soul. Though she was busy, her smile seemed to promise that we would talk once she was free. I smiled back and returned to Maaji's room, feeling more at ease.

After servingher dinner and eating my own, I tucked her into bed. But my anticipation to meet the nurse again made it impossible for me to sit still. I paced the room, glancing at the clock every few minutes, waiting for her to come.

Finally, at 11:30 PM, she arrived. My heart leaped with childlike excitement as I welcomed her. She noticed right away that I wasn't holding my usual Sai Satcharitra book. "Where's your book today? Are you not reading tonight?" she asked with a gentle smile.

I realized then that in my eagerness to talk to her, I had completely forgotten to bring the book. Embarrassed, I admitted, "I wanted to talk to you, so I left it behind."

At that moment, someone entered the room with two cups of tea. Seeing the puzzled look on my face, the nurse explained, "I thought we could chat over tea tonight. It helps me stay awake during my night shifts." Her thoughtfulness touched me deeply.

She could see the questions written all over my face and smiled, urging me, "Tell me, what's on your mind?"

I poured my heart out to her, recounting the incident with Sai Baba's Vibhuti and how my daughter's actions mirrored what her daughter had done with Ayappa's Vibhuti.

Her face turned somber as tears welled up in her eyes. She confessed, "My daughter is severely autistic. That incident brought hope and positivity into our lives, something we desperately needed."

Hearing this, I felt an unexplainable connection with her. My tears started flowing as I shared, "My daughter also has autism, though hers is mild."

She nodded, her expression softening. "I sensed it when I saw her the other day at the hospital. I wanted to help you, but I wasn't sure if you'd be okay with me bringing it up."

At that moment, something shifted. We both embraced, our tears flowing freely, as though we were two souls navigating the same stormy sea, finding solace in each other's presence.

After some time, we wiped our tears and composed ourselves. She then shared something that felt like an answer to my prayers. "There's a wonderful Special Education Centre nearby. Your daughter could benefit greatly from it."

At that moment, everything became clear. Sai Baba had sent her into my life to guide me when I needed it most. Gratitude filled my heart, both for her and for Sai Baba's divine intervention.

Determined, I resolved to visit the center the very next day. With a heart full of hope and a newfound connection, I thanked her and silently prayed to Sai Baba, knowing this was just the beginning of a new journey for my daughter and me.

Chapter 10
The Second Chance At Parenthood

I was the happiest person on Earth the day my daughter's therapy started at the Special Education Centre. After months of searching and endless prayers, we found a place where she could be nurtured, understood, and supported. Her therapist was a remarkable woman, patient yet firm, who believed in my daughter even before we could fully grasp the potential hidden within her.

It felt as though the universe had finally started to shift in our favour. The boulders that once seemed insurmountable began to roll away, clearing a path we had only dreamed of walking. My daughter began progressing—not in small, hesitant steps, but by leaps and bounds. Each milestone she achieved felt like a little miracle, a divine reassurance that we were on the right path.

And then, the unthinkable happened. My daughter, once struggling to find her place in the world, gained admission to one of the best schools in our locality. The joy and pride that filled my heart on that day were indescribable. Life, which had once been clouded with doubt and despair, was now glowing with a newfound positivity.

As a family, we began to heal. The walls of stress that had built up around us started to crumble. We laughed more often, shared more moments, and rediscovered the importance of cherishing the little things—things we had forgotten amid the chaos. Weekend picnics, silly games at home, and bedtime stories became our sanctuary. With every shared smile and warm hug, we reclaimed our happiness and peace.

Time passed, and with each passing month, my daughter's growth was nothing short of extraordinary. She excelled in her studies, surprising her teachers and classmates alike. She wasn't just keeping up; she was thriving. Accolades poured in for her academic achievements and her co-curricular pursuits. My heart swelled with pride every time someone recognized her potential, and for a moment, I believed life had given me all I could ever ask for.

But life, as unpredictable as it is, always has a way of leading you to the next chapter. Deep within, I felt a yearning—one I couldn't ignore. After this rollercoaster journey of struggles and triumphs, of depression and motivation, I longed for something more. Or rather, someone. I realized I wanted to bring a sibling into my daughter's life—a playmate, a companion, someone who would never judge her but would love her unconditionally.

More than that, I needed this for myself. The desire to have another child was more than just a wish; it was a longing to heal my soul completely, to fill a space in my heart that still felt incomplete. And so, with my husband by my side, we began our quest to welcome another child into our lives.

The first step was to consult a gynaecologist. I remember feeling a blend of nervous excitement as I walked into her clinic. She listened patiently to our dreams and prescribed essential medicines to prepare my body for this journey. With hope and positivity as our guiding lights, my husband and I embarked on this new adventure, eager to hold a little bundle of joy once again.

But life didn't make it easy. Days turned into months, and months into years, yet there was no sign of success. Three long years passed, marked by disappointment after disappointment. Each negative result felt like a dagger to my heart. What was I doing wrong? Why couldn't I conceive? The questions haunted me day and night, but the answers eluded me.

Visits to the doctor became a routine part of my life. Each consultation ended with the same vague assurances, but no concrete answers. My hope began to waver, and yet, deep within, I refused to let go of the dream.

Amid all this turmoil, I clung to my faith. Every Thursday, I would visit the temple, offering food to the needy as part of my ritual. It was my way of staying connected to the divine, of seeking strength when I felt weakest.

One such Thursday, as I sat reading the newspaper, a small advertisement caught my eye. It wasn't even on the front page—just a small corner featuring a picture of Sai Baba and an event announcement. I turned the page, only to find a full-page ad for a hospital specializing in infertility treatments. The headline boldly claimed that they had resolved cases where all hope seemed lost.

Something stirred inside me—a quiet but insistent voice urging me to act. It felt like a sign, a message from Sai Baba himself. Without a moment's hesitation, I picked up the phone and called the hospital. As I dialled the number, my hands trembled with a mix of fear and anticipation. Was this the answer I had been waiting for?

I booked an appointment with the doctor, my heart brimming with hope once again. It was as though the universe, after years of testing me, was finally pointing me toward the light.

⁂

Chapter 11
Battling The Odds with Silent Courage

The day of my appointment finally arrived. Nervous yet hopeful, I made my way to the hospital to meet the doctor. She was a gentle, soft-spoken lady in her late 40s, her kind eyes and profound smile radiating warmth. The moment I stepped into her cabin, I felt a sense of comfort, as though I was in the presence of someone who truly cared.

I handed her my stack of medical reports and shared the details of my previous consultations with other doctors. I also spoke about my elder daughter, who had been the centre of my world and my inspiration to keep going. Dr. Rita carefully examined everything, flipping through the reports with a meticulous eye.

After a while, she looked up, her expression calm yet empathetic. "You know, my dear," she began, "sometimes we do everything right, but the time hasn't come for us to receive what we want. That's when we feel stressed and lose hope. But always remember this—it is well said that 'Man proposes, God disposes,' and He does so for our good. Believe in Him and start your journey again, this time with renewed hope and positivity."

Her words were like a soothing balm to my troubled soul. Her wisdom, combined with her gentle tone, reignited a flicker of courage within me. She prescribed some medicines and laid out a plan for me to follow. I left her office with a mix of hope and determination, ready to give my dream another chance.

For the next six months, I followed every instruction Dr. Rita had given me. I adhered to the treatment plan religiously, clinging to the hope that this time, the outcome would be different. But as the months passed, my success rate remained painfully at zero.

Impatience began to creep in. Years had already slipped through my fingers, and I couldn't bear the thought of losing more time. One evening, overwhelmed by frustration and sorrow, I returned to Dr. Rita's clinic. This time, I couldn't hold back my emotions. Tears welled up in my eyes as I poured my heart out to her. She listened patiently, her calm demeanor never wavering.

After a pause, she said, "Let's go for an internal checkup. It will give us more clarity."

I agreed, desperate for answers. The checkup was done, and the wait for the report was nerve-wracking. The day I was to receive the results, I sat in the hospital lobby, drowning in a sea of negative thoughts. What if the results brought more bad news? What if this was the end of the road for me?

Suddenly, my name was called. The nurse informed me that the doctor already had my report and asked me to proceed to her cabin. My heart pounded as I walked down the corridor, each step heavier than the last.

When I entered Dr. Rita's cabin, I saw her studying the report intently. Her face was serious, her brows furrowed in concern. My stomach churned as I sat down, unable to read her expression. Summoning the courage to speak, I asked, "Is everything okay, Doctor?"

She took a deep breath, avoiding eye contact for a moment before she finally said, "The news is not good." Her voice was heavy with concern. "There's an issue with your uterus wall. It seems the placenta is unable to adhere to it, which is significantly reducing your chances of conception."

Her words hit me like a thunderbolt. It felt as though the floor beneath me had disappeared. My mind went blank, and my body felt weak and dizzy. A million questions swirled in my head, but none of them made it to my lips. I sat there in stunned silence, struggling to process the devastating news.

Finally, in a trembling voice, I managed to ask, "Does this mean I'll never be able to conceive? Should I give up on this dream?"

Dr. Rita's gaze softened. "I'm not saying you should give up," she said gently. "You've been through so much, and the stress you've endured has taken a toll on your body. Stress can wreak havoc on our hormones, and that might be contributing to this condition. But while the chances are weak, they aren't zero. If it's God's will, it will happen. Don't lose hope just yet."

I nodded, unable to say anything more. My heart was heavy, and my eyes brimmed with tears as I left her cabin. I noticed a shadow of sadness on Dr. Rita's face too, as though she shared my pain. Over the months, she had become more than just a doctor—she had become a confidante, someone who genuinely cared about my journey.

When I reached home, I chose to keep the news to myself. I didn't tell my husband or anyone else. I couldn't bear the thought of bringing his hopes crashing down, not after everything we'd already been through.

But bottling up my emotions came at a price. The grief weighed on me like a heavy cloud, seeping into every corner of my life. Though I tried to put on a brave face, those who loved me could sense that something was amiss. My silence created an aura of negativity that was impossible to hide.

I felt like I was trapped in a cycle of sorrow, with no one to share my burden. Yet, amidst the darkness, a tiny spark of hope refused to be extinguished. Maybe, just maybe, the next chapter of my story would hold a miracle.

Chapter 12
A Divine Encounter

It was a usual Thursday morning, and as part of my cherished ritual, I was preparing food to offer to Sai Baba. Thursdays had always been special to me, a day dedicated to devotion and service, a day that filled me with a sense of peace amidst the chaos of life. Over the years, I had also started working at the center where my daughter used to go for her therapies. The plan for the day was simple—complete my Sai Baba pooja, prepare the prasad, pack food to give to the needy as part of my Thursday routine, and then head to work.

The pooja was as serene as ever. I carefully packed the prasad and the food, said goodbye to my in-laws, and stepped out of the house. The atmosphere outside was vibrant. In our locality, Thursdays often witnessed the grand *Sai Palki* procession—a parade of Sai Baba's idol carried by his devotees from the Sai temple, accompanied by chants and music. That day too, the Palki procession was passing by the road near our apartment. The air was thick with devotion, the rhythmic chants of "Sai Ram" resonating deeply in my heart. I stood there calmly, waiting for the procession to pass so I could proceed to work.

As I stood, I instinctively started looking around for someone to whom I could offer the food and prasad. It was my way of sharing Sai Baba's blessings with those in need. And then, it happened—a moment that still feels like a dream.

I turned around, and there he was—a young boy standing right in front of me as if he had appeared out of nowhere. I remember his face vividly even now. He was lean, no older than 19 or 20, with a long face adorned with a bright *Chandan (sandalwood)* and vermillion tilak on his forehead. He wore a simple dhoti-kurta, with a yellow cloth draped around his neck. There was something extraordinary about him—an aura so magnetic and positive that it left me spellbound.

"Didi, how are you?" he asked, his voice warm and familiar, as though we had known each other forever. For a moment, I was taken aback. Why should I respond to a complete stranger? But then, a memory flashed in my mind—a haunting recollection of the day I had ignored an old man in the market, only to regret it later. I dreaded making the same mistake again.

Gathering myself, I replied, "I'm good. Are you with the Palki?"

"Yes," he said, smiling. "I was in the Palki when I saw you, so I came here to meet you."

His words were strange, almost otherworldly, but there was something about his presence that put me at ease. I smiled back and asked if he would like to take the prasad and the food I had packed. He accepted it gently, saying, "Didi, thank you, I was very hungry. Because of the procession, I couldn't eat anything since morning."

Hearing this, I felt a deep sense of relief and happiness. I was glad that the food had reached someone who truly needed it. I greeted him with a heartfelt *namaste* and was about to leave when his next words stopped me in my tracks.

"Didi, you are worried about having a child, right?"

I froze. How could he possibly know that? I stared at him, stunned. I had never seen this boy before, and he didn't seem to belong to our locality. Yet, he had touched upon the one wound I had kept hidden from the world. Tears welled up in my eyes as he continued speaking, his voice filled with compassion.

"I know you cry a lot," he said softly. "Don't do that. Your good days have begun, and much happiness is on its way to you."

He paused for a moment, as if to let his words sink in, and then added, "Within a year and a half, you will have a child in your arms. Believe me, and have faith in Sai Baba. He always protects his children and does what is best for them. Be prepared for a lot of joy ahead. Tell your husband not to worry either. With Baba's *kripa*, everything will be fine."

By now, I was sobbing uncontrollably. His words felt like comfort to my aching soul like Sai Baba himself was speaking to me through this boy. I didn't dare blink, afraid that he might disappear if I looked away for even a second. I stood there, overwhelmed, my heart swelling with a mix of disbelief, gratitude, and hope.

Finally, I gathered the courage to ask, "Bhaiya, are you going to Shirdi?"

To my surprise, he replied, "I live there. I came here for some work."

Something within me urged me to offer him more. "Can I give you something to offer as prasad in Shirdi?" I asked.

He smiled and said, "Okay. We are going to make *khichdi today for prasad and would carry it on our journey*. We already have rice, but if you want, you can give me some *daal* (lentils). We don't have enough of that."

I nodded eagerly and said, "Please wait here. Don't go anywhere. I'll be back in five minutes."

With those words, I turned and rushed toward my house. My heart was pounding, not from the running but from the fear of losing him. It felt as though my entire being was racing against time.

Chapter 13
The Mystical Prasad Connection

That moment was chaotic, with a whirlwind of emotions and actions. I rang the bell at home several times, my heart racing with a strange sense of urgency. Papaji opened the door, surprised to see me standing there. "Have you not left for office?" he asked, his voice tinged with curiosity and concern. Without answering directly, I hastily said, "I will tell you everything, Papaji. Just give me some time."

I rushed to the kitchen, searching frantically for the packet of daal (lentils) the boy had requested. To my dismay, I found only half a packet. The clock seemed to be ticking faster as I darted to my almirah, grabbing a ₹500 note and a 1-rupee coin. Clutching the note, coin, and daal packet, I hurried down the stairs, my mind fervently praying that the boy wouldn't vanish into thin air before I reached him.

When I finally reached downstairs, gasping for breath, a wave of relief washed over me as I saw the boy still standing there, smiling serenely. His smile held a strange warmth, almost as if it carried a sense of reassurance. I handed him the half-packet of daal and the money, apologizing, "I didn't have much daal. Please accept this money and buy more for the prasad."

He accepted it with a gentle smile and said, "Didi, I am going to Shirdi right now with this Palki. You must visit Shirdi sometime. When everything in your life is good again, when you're happy and satisfied, I'll come back. And when I do, I'd love to have a cup of tea with you."

His words struck a chord deep within me, leaving me both puzzled and hopeful. I smiled back and said, "You're most welcome. Come anytime." I even pointed out my apartment and told him my flat number. He nodded and started walking toward the Palki. I stood there, watching him until he disappeared into the procession, unwilling to lose sight of him.

As I turned to leave for the office, a sudden realization hit me—I hadn't given him the 1-rupee coin. It felt important as if it held some unspoken significance. Without thinking, I ran back toward the procession, searching for the boy amidst the sea of people. But he was nowhere to be found. Desperate, I ran toward the Palki, where Sai Baba's idol was placed. A Panditji sat nearby, chanting softly.

"Panditji," I asked, my voice trembling, "there was a boy here, part of this procession. Where is he?"

The priest looked at me with a puzzled expression and said, "There are so many people in the procession. How can I know about one boy?"

Feeling a pang of disappointment, my eyes wandered to the idol, and there, near Sai Baba's feet, I saw the half-packet of daal I had given the boy. My heart skipped a beat. "Panditji, who kept this packet here?" I asked.

He shrugged and replied, "So many people come and offer things. Someone must have kept it. I don't remember."

I pressed on, my mind refusing to let go of the mystery. "When is this Palki going to Shirdi? Are you going to cook khichdi today? Should I bring more daal?"

The Panditji's answer shook me to my core. "Who said we are going to Shirdi? This is the temple's Palki. It stays here and doesn't go anywhere. And no, we're not cooking khichdi today. We will keep the daal in the temple's ration. Everything offered here is Sai's wish."

His words left me speechless. The realization dawned on me like a flash of lightning. I placed the 1-rupee coin in the pooja thali before the idol, touched Baba's feet, and left for the office. My mind was a whirlwind of thoughts and emotions. Who was that boy? Where did he go? Could it have been Baba himself?

Memories of a similar encounter years ago, when an old woman had vanished from a temple, resurfaced in my mind.

I reached the office in a daze, my heart heavy with unanswered questions. The divine encounter had left me awestruck, yet I couldn't find solace until I uncovered the truth.

The day unfolded as usual, with work keeping me busy. It wasn't until lunchtime that the morning's events came rushing back to me. As I opened my lunchbox, the boy's words echoed in my mind. "Why did he ask only for daal? If the Palki wasn't going to Shirdi, then what journey was he talking about? And why was he supposed to cook khichdi?"

The questions lingered as I ate my lunch, each bite bringing back fragments of the morning. Unable to contain my curiosity, I returned to my desk after lunch and opened my browser. Almost instinctively, my fingers typed into the search bar: "Is khichdi offered as prasad at Shirdi?"

The answer sent a chill down my spine: "Khichdi is one of the primary prasad items offered every Thursday, as it is considered to be Sai Baba's favourite dish."

A wave of gratitude and awe washed over me. Tears welled up in my eyes as the realization hit me—Baba himself had come to take the khichdi from my hands.

The boy's words replayed in my mind: "When everything will be good in your life, and you are happy and satisfied, I will come again. I love tea, so I will come and have tea with you."

I closed my eyes, a sense of peace and gratitude enveloping me. Sai Baba had once again shown his divine presence in my life, reminding me of his boundless love and blessings.

Chapter 14
The Awaited Blessings

Time has a mysterious way of unfolding its blessings, often in ways we least expect. It had been nearly eight months since that unforgettable morning when I had met the strange yet divine boy. His words lingered in my heart, filling me with both curiosity and faith. *"When everything falls into place, when you are happy and content, I will return. And then, I will have tea with you."* His words had echoed in my mind many times, and though life had moved on, a part of me was always waiting, hoping, and believing.

Eight months later, something truly miraculous happened— One morning, I felt an unusual wave of emotions wash over me. There was no apparent reason, but I sensed a change within. A few days passed, and a little voice inside nudged me to take a test. My heart pounded as I held the pregnancy kit in my hands, waiting for the result. And then, there it was—two bold, unmistakable lines. I was pregnant! something I never thought possible.

Given my medical history and the anomalies with my uterine wall, the chances of conceiving naturally were slim.

When I visited my doctor, she flipped through my medical reports, her eyebrows furrowing in disbelief. "I am so happy this happened," she admitted, scanning the ultrasound images once more. "Medically, this was difficult but... here you are, perfectly pregnant." She hugged me tightly. Tears welled up in my eyes again. This was no coincidence; I smiled through my tears. "It's Baba," I whispered, clutching my belly.

The joy that filled our home was indescribable. It was as though the universe had chosen this exact moment to bless us with another beautiful soul. My husband

and I had longed for this, and now, as if Sai Baba himself had orchestrated it, our prayers were answered. The pregnancy was smooth, and each passing day brought us closer to welcoming our newest family member.

And then, after months of waiting, the day finally arrived. With my husband by my side, I brought a beautiful baby girl into this world. The moment I held her in my arms, I felt an overwhelming surge of love, gratitude, and something unexplainable—something divine. It was as if she had carried a piece of Baba's blessings with her.

But Baba's grace did not stop there. Three days after our daughter's birth, my husband received a phone call. Half-asleep from the exhaustion of the past few days, he almost ignored it. But something made him answer - "Hello?" What followed was a moment of sheer astonishment. It was the job offer he had been yearning for— My husband, who had been struggling for years to secure a better job, received an offer he could only dream of. It was a position in Bangalore, a role that recognized his skills and potential, and a city we had long considered moving to. The timing was impeccable. Just when we were preparing to grow our family, life was making space for us to thrive.

With his new job, a new sense of stability settled into our lives. The worries of the past seemed to fade, replaced by excitement for the future. We moved to Bangalore, embraced the new opportunities that came our way and felt the presence of Sai Baba's blessings in every little moment. The challenges that once seemed insurmountable were now stepping stones toward a brighter path.

In another corner of our lives, another transformation was taking place. Our elder daughter, who had always faced struggles due to autism, began to blossom in ways we had never imagined. Her academic progress became evident, and she started taking strides in her learning journey. The small victories—reading a paragraph on her own, understanding mathematical concepts, expressing her thoughts more clearly—became our greatest joys.

Beyond academics, her independence was growing. The little girl who once needed constant assistance was now managing her routines with confidence. She was coping well at school, forming friendships, and engaging in social settings that once overwhelmed her. It felt as though something divine was guiding her, making her path smoother, making her life easier.

This was Baba's way of telling us that we were under his watchful eyes, that he had heard every silent prayer, seen every struggle, and finally decided to bless us with what we had longed for.

Despite all these blessings, there was one thought that never left my mind—the promise the boy had made. *"When you are happy....//..................... and content, I will return and have tea with you."* Life had indeed become beautiful, yet that moment has not arrived.

Somewhere deep inside, I know that this isn't the end of the blessings. If Sai Baba has given me so much, if his presence is transforming my life in unimaginable ways, then surely, there is still more to come. The journey isn't over. There are still more miracles waiting to unfold.

I wake up every morning with gratitude in my heart, knowing that my family is thriving, that my husband is finally content, that my elder daughter is overcoming her challenges, and that my little one is growing up in a home filled with love and positivity. And yet, I find myself glancing toward the door every now and then, half-expecting to see that familiar face, that gentle smile, that mysterious yet comforting presence.

Maybe he will come tomorrow, or maybe he will take his time. But I know one thing for sure—when he does, I will welcome him with open arms, serve him a warm cup of tea, and thank him for the countless blessings he has showered upon my life. Until then, I wait with faith, with love, and with the unshakable belief that the best is yet to come.

www.ingramcontent.com/pod-product-compliance
Lightning Source LLC
LaVergne TN
LVHW061557070526
838199LV00077B/7089